T0051700

ÀLEX NOVIALS · EVA PALOMAR

TUTANKHAMUN

The tale of the child pharaoh and the discovery of his tomb

ORANGE
M·O·S·Q·U·I·T·O

"The most wonderful day of my life"

HELLO, MY FRIENDS! My name is Howard Carter and I'm an archaeologist. I was in Egypt more than a hundred years ago looking for the hidden treasures of the ancient pharaohs. The year 1922 was rushing by and we had already been working for several months without finding anything. We were quite discouraged ... In fact, we were preparing to leave our excavation in the Valley of the Kings.

BUT WE MADE ONE LAST EFFORT. And the moment we had so hoped for arrived! On the 4th of November, some mysterious steps that descended into the earth appeared. And then a door with its seals intact. Could this really be the tomb of a king? Behind the door was a long passage filled to the roof with rubble. It took us a day and a half to clear it! Then a second sealed door appeared. We had no idea what would be inside...

CAN YOU IMAGINE HOW EXCITED WE WERE? I made a small hole in the door, enough to be able to place a candle inside. At first, I couldn't see anything because warm air escaping from inside made the flame flicker. But when my eyes grew accustomed to the dark, I began to see hundreds of treasures piled one on top of the other. There were chests, beds, statues, and strange animals. And gold glinting everywhere!

FOR A MOMENT, I WAS LOST FOR WORDS. It was so much more than I could ever have dreamed of! Then Lord Carnarvon, who was the wealthy patron of the excavation, asked me nervously: "Can you see anything?" I could only reply: "Yes, wonderful things." Do you want to know what the fantastic discovery of Tutankhamun's tomb was like? Come with me and I'll explain all the secrets of the ancient Egyptians ... I'm sure you'll be amazed!

For Artau and Mònica, for the stolen hours.
But now we have a new tale to tell.
ÀLEX

To my parents for their support and infinite kindness.
Thank you for always being there.
EVA

Published in 2022 by Orange Mosquito
An Imprint of Welbeck Children's Limited
part of Welbeck Publishing Group.
Based in London and Sydney.
www.welbeckpublishing.com

In collaboration with Mosquito Books Barcelona S.L.

© Mosquito Books Barcelona, SL 2022
Text © Àlex Novials 2022
Illustration © Eva Palomar 2022
Translation: Maria White
Publisher: Margaux Durigon
UK editor: Jo Hanks
Production: Jess Brisley

All rights reserved. No part of this publication may be reproduced, stored in a retrieval system,
or transmitted in any form or by any means, electronically, mechanical, photocopying, recording
or otherwise, without the prior permission of the copyright owners and the publishers.

ISBN: 9781914519581
eISBN: 9781914519598

Printed in Spain
10 9 8 7 6 5 4 3 2 1

Fascinated by the pharaohs

I suppose you should probably ask yourselves how I actually arrived in Egypt. I was born in the year 1873 in a small town called Swaffham in the northeast of England. I was the youngest of eleven brothers and our father was an artist. I suffered from poor health so instead of going to school they educated me at home. And as I showed a talent for drawing, Papa taught me art from a very young age.

I had the opportunity to visit Lord William Amherst's collection of antiquities to draw the items. That wealthy landowner had a room full of beautiful statues of Egyptian gods, fantastic parchment scrolls, and other archaeological treasures. That ancient civilization captured my imagination completely!

1873. The year of my birth

1883. I discover the art of ancient Egypt

1890. I arrive in Egypt to work as an artist

In Egypt at last!

I arrived in Egypt when I was 17 years old. I had no experience but, even so, the famous archaeologist Percy Newberry hired me as an artist. His team was excavating in the tombs of Beni Hassan. There were some magnificent paintings that portrayed scenes from the times of the pharaohs, and I had to copy them. As you can imagine, I loved my work...

At last, I had achieved my dream of seeing all those wonderful antiquities in person! A year later, I worked in the ancient city of Amarna with another very famous archaeologist, Flinders Petrie, and then with Édouard Naville in the temple of Hatshepsut in Deir el-Bahri. I was so lucky, wasn't I?

Learning every day

I hadn't studied at university, but I was very observant, and I learned very quickly from the experts around me. As well as that, I was a tireless worker and quite hardy: I could solve any problem with my own hands! Oh, and I learned Arabic to be able to understand the Egyptian workers..

When I was 25 years old, they appointed me Chief Inspector of Monuments for Upper Egypt. It's a great title, isn't it? They say that my work was excellent: we discovered lots of tombs and I also managed to capture many grave robbers and bring them to justice.

1899. I work for the antiquities department

1907. I meet Lord Carnarvon

1922. I discover Tutankhamun's tomb

Just my luck

In 1905 some tourists tried to enter a monument in Sakkarah without buying tickets and hit the guard who tried to stop them. I insisted the tourists pay and said the guards should defend themselves if they were attacked. There was a fight and the tourists complained. In the end, I had to resign from my post.

I had three difficult years
I made a living selling drawings and watercolors to tourists... But my real wish was to lead an archaeological excavation in the Valley of the Kings, the place where many pharaohs had been buried. In the year 1907, I met Lord Carnarvon, a wealthy English aristocrat. He became a fan of antiquities when his doctor recommended that he spend his winters in Egypt for his health. He would become my patron.

Who was Tutankhamun?

It is now exactly 3,354 years since Tutankhamun was the most important person in Egypt. He was only nine, but he was already pharaoh, the king of a great empire. His reign was not long or distinguished, but his tomb would make him the most famous pharaoh in the world.

HE WAS BORN DURING THE NEW KINGDOM,
a period in which Egypt was a powerful empire. It shows in the magnificence of its culture: they had spectacular works of art. He was the son of Pharaoh Akhenaten and his mother was also his aunt! This now seems very strange to us, but it was common in those days for a king to marry women in his own family. The mother of Tutankhamun is called The Younger Lady because we don't know her name.

THE REIGN OF TUTANKHAMUN'S FATHER
was complicated. It turned out that he suddenly wanted to change the country's religion. He banned Egyptians from worshipping the many gods they had always believed in and forced them to worship only Aten, the sun god. As you can imagine, most people were not happy about it...

WHEN OUR MAIN CHARACTER WAS BORN
around the year 1342 BC, they called him Tutankhaten which meant "living image of Aten." His father soon died, and he took the throne when he was only about eight or nine years old. As the new pharaoh was still a child, power was really managed by the Grand Vizier Ay, who had been advisor to his father, and Horemheb, a powerful general in the army.

TUTANKHAMUN IMMEDIATELY MARRIED
his half-sister Ankhesenpaaten who was a few years older than him. She was the daughter of his father and his principal wife, Queen Nefertiti. A year after the wedding, the pharaoh re-established the cult of the traditional gods and changed his name: Amun was the new king of the gods, so now he was Tutankhamun!

THE TRUTH IS THAT WE KNOW VERY LITTLE
about Tutankhamun's life. His father fell into disgrace, and a lot of documents about the reign of Tutankhamun were also destroyed. There are many pieces missing from the puzzle! What we do know through the study of his mummy is that the king was fragile and had a serious illness: his bones crumbled easily. He also had a curved spine and deformed feet, so he needed a stick to walk. As if that wasn't enough, he had malaria, a very dangerous disease. He died unexpectedly when he was 19 years old. What a short life.

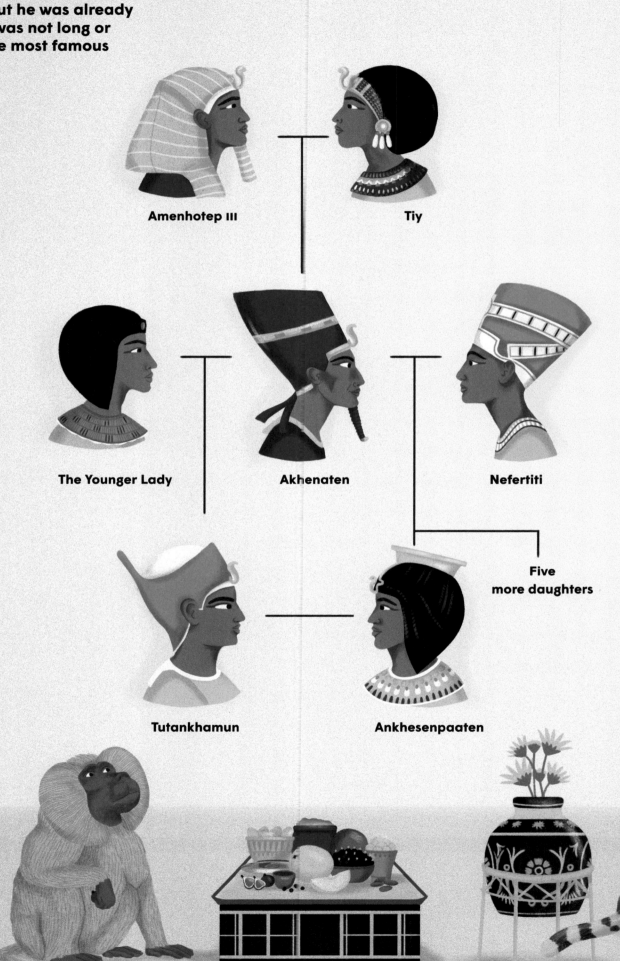

Amenhotep III

Tiy

The Younger Lady

Akhenaten

Nefertiti

Five more daughters

Tutankhamun

Ankhesenpaaten

The pharaoh, an all-powerful king

Egyptian civilization lasted more than 3,000 years. During this long period of time, the pharaohs always occupied the most important position in society. They were considered intermediaries between the gods and men, so their work was very important.

SYMBOLS OF POWER

The pharaoh's crown was red and white, representing the two halves of his kingdom: Upper and Lower Egypt. In his hand, he held a crook and flail, the tool used to thresh grains. They were symbols of his duty: to protect his people and ensure the fertility of the land.

THE PHARAOH WAS RESPONSIBLE for leading the country and safeguarding its prosperity. He was the Supreme Chief of the army, passed laws, and decreed the taxes that his subjects had to pay, and was aided by many public servants who obeyed him without complaint. To ensure that the gods were happy, he ordered the construction of temples and enormous statues and made sure the priests always carried out appropriate ceremonies.

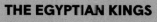

They could marry several women at the same time, but only the first wife was queen. She also had an important function, but women took power as pharaoh on very few occasions. The most famous were Hatshepsut and Cleopatra VII. After the death of a pharaoh, his eldest son would normally take the throne—if he had one, of course. As you will see, this didn't happen in the case of Tutankhamun.

TUTANKHAMUN WIELDED A LOT OF POWER, but he also had many responsibilities. It wasn't an easy job, was it? And if that wasn't enough, pharaohs were considered sons of Ra, the sun god. His work also included upholding justice, the truth, and order in the universe. The Egyptians thought that when their kings died, they joined Osiris, the god who reigned in the afterlife. In other words, once dead, they were worshipped as gods.

What do hieroglyphs say?

The Egyptians were one of the first peoples to describe things in writing—more than 5,000 years ago. For a long time, hieroglyphs were used to leave clear records of their customs, history, and beliefs.

CHILDREN BEGAN TO GO TO THE TEMPLE SCHOOLS at the age of five, but serious learning began at the age of nine. They learned to write by copying the same texts time and time again. And as papyrus was expensive, they did it on stones or pieces of broken pottery!

THEY BELIEVED THAT WRITING was a gift from Thoth, the wisest god of all. They developed a complete system to represent sounds and words: drawings of birds and other animals, trees and plants, people and parts of the human body, tools and weapons, buildings and boats ... Around the year 2900 BC, hieroglyphs were already well defined, and they continued to use them for more than 3,300 years. No other writing system has been used for so long!

TO US, READING AND WRITING seems so normal, but in those times, it was a skill reserved for very few people. It was only taught to scribes who committed to writing professionally. The profession usually passed from father to son, and it was reserved exclusively for boys. Girls were forbidden from doing it. How unfair!

THEY STUDIED FOR A LONG TIME: it took twelve years to become a good scribe. But those who mastered the challenge were well-respected people in Egyptian society. They were part of the royal court and enjoyed a good salary and other interesting advantages. They didn't pay tax, and they didn't have to serve in the army or take part in the building of temples and tombs. How lucky!

THE SCRIBES sat on the floor with their legs crossed. They stretched their skirts across their knees, to serve as a table. They used a reed brush, and the ink was placed in two holes on a wooden palette. The black ink was for writing and the red for correcting. Just as it is now!

How they made papyrus

The process of making paper with the fibers of papyrus plants was a delicate task and required a lot of time. (There was a good reason why papyrus was so expensive!) The sheets were stuck together, and that's how scrolls were created to write whole books. In other words, instead of turning pages to read them, you had to keep unrolling a single long document. The record is held by the Harris papyrus which is 134.5 feet long!

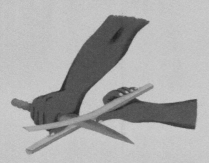

1 The green outer stem of the papyrus plant was peeled off. Then the white inside was cut into long and very thin strips of around 16 inches long.

2 Lots of strips were laid together on a hard, flat surface, all in the same direction. Then they placed another layer on top, but this time the strips were placed in the opposite direction.

3 They put a very diluted glue on top which they extracted from other plants that we don't know about. With this ingredient, they managed to stick the two layers of reeds together forming one sheet.

4 They beat the pulp with a wooden mallet and then pressed it with a weight for a few days. When the fibers were dry, they made the papyrus smooth with a wooden or marble tool. Then it was ready to write on!

The gift of the nile

The Nile is the second longest river on Earth, just a little behind the Amazon. From its sources in the heart of Africa, it runs for almost 400 miles until it flows into the Mediterranean. For the inhabitants of ancient Egypt, its waters were a real blessing.

MOST OF THE COUNTRY was an inhospitable desert that they called Deshret, the "Red Land." Life was impossible there! However, a fragile strip extended along the banks of the Nile which could be cultivated: this was Kemet, the "Black Land." The people who lived there saw that the waters rose and flooded the closest fields in the month of July. Four months later, the river returned to its course and left the fields covered in silt, a fine, blackish clay. They noticed that if they planted seeds in those fields, the plants grew rapidly and provided a lot of produce. What a great gift!

THE NILE was not only used to water farmers' fields. It was also the main communication and transport route for the country.

BUT THE FLOODWATER WAS NOT ALWAYS THE SAME. Some years, when it rained a great deal in the center of Africa, the water rose excessively. On other occasions, the floodwaters were hardly noticeable. So, they built small dams to collect the water and opened canals to carry it to distant fields.

It was very hard work, but the results made it worthwhile: with wells and dikes, the green blanket of plants extended from Aswan, the first cataract (a shallow and rocky stretch of water), to the sea. And so, the Egyptian civilisation was born!

HONOR THE GODS

The ancient Egyptians had many gods and goddesses, one for every place and every situation. They believed that the gods ruled over everything, from family life to the movement of the stars, and that the waters of the Nile were the reward they received for worshipping them. That was why religion was so important! Everyone had a small sanctuary in the garden or an altar in the house for offerings and rituals.

THE FIRST PHARAOH. The Egyptians lived in increasingly larger groups. The first cities, such as Memphis, Abydos, and Naqada, appeared. Much later, some of them joined together and formed small kingdoms. Eventually, there were only two large kingdoms: Lower Egypt in the Nile delta and Upper Egypt in the south of the country. Five thousand years ago, a powerful king from the south conquered the north. He was called Narmer, and he became the first pharaoh of a united Egypt!

ENOUGH TIME FOR EVERYTHING. They cultivated wheat and barley, for bread; onions, beans, lentils, vegetables, and fruit as well as plants like flax and papyrus to make their clothes and the scrolls they wrote on. As they had more food than they needed, some Egyptians could do other work. There were craftsmen, musicians, and priests. In the months when the Nile flooded their fields, farmers helped with the building of great temples and pyramids.

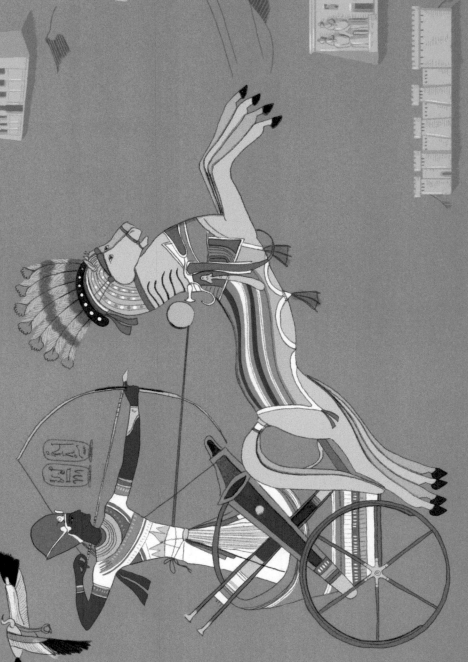

Life after death

The ancient Egyptians believed that the god Osiris ruled the afterlife. The dead traveled to this other world, the Duat, to enjoy a new life of eternal happiness. But first they had to pass some tests to show that they were worthy of it...

THE JUDGMENT OF THE GODS. In the upper section, the great gods preside over the ceremony, seated on their thrones. In front of them is a small table with offerings.

THE CENTRAL FIGURE. The deceased was named Ani and was a royal scribe, a very important post. His wife Tutu, a priestess of the god Amun, accompanies him. She carries a sistrum in her hand, a rattle that was used in dances and sacred ceremonies.

A SOUL WITH WINGS. This bird is the ba (the part of the soul representing personality) of the deceased. It allows the deceased to come and go, flying from his mummy to the kingdom of the dead.

EVERYONE WATCHES. Near the scales is the god of destiny, Shai. Behind him is his wife, Meskhenet, the goddess of childbirth. When a baby was born, she breathed life—ka (this part of the soul was considered to be a person's spirit)—into it. She is accompanied by Renenutet, the goddess of nourishment.

The belief in an afterlife was very important to them. It wasn't that they were afraid of death, they just loved life ... They wanted to go on forever! But reaching eternity was not an easy task. You may already know that they prepared the dead in a very special way, as you will see in this book. Then they buried them with all the belongings they would need in the afterlife, including food so that they wouldn't go hungry along the way. The wealthiest people had fabulous tombs built, particularly the pharaohs.

The Book of the Dead was a manual full of magic spells, with all the steps that had to be followed for a successful final journey. Would you like to know what's happening in this drawing?

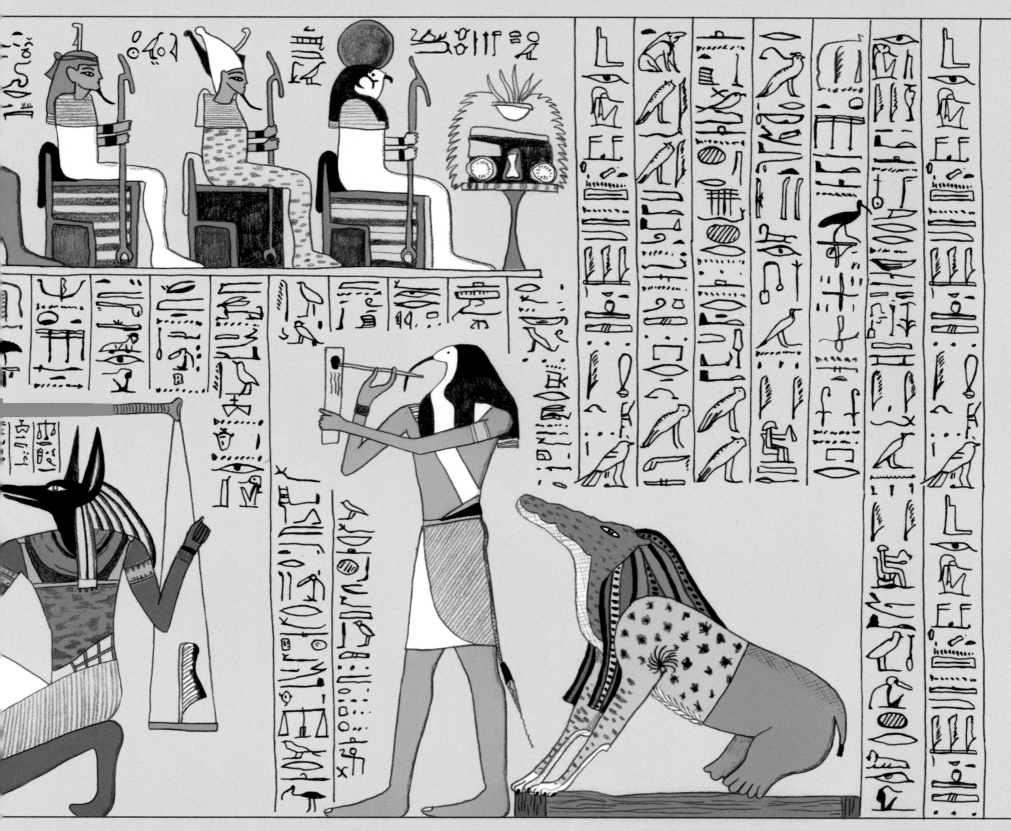

THE WEIGHING OF THE SOUL. The heart of the deceased is placed in a dish on the scales and on the other is the feather of truth. Anubis, with the head of a jackal, is responsible for weighing it to see if the deceased has behaved well during his life on earth: he is the god of death and mummification.

THE DIVINE SCRIBE. Thoth, the god with an ibis head, notes the result. For some things he is the god of wisdom and hieroglyphic writing. As the scales remain balanced, Thoth proclaims there is no evil in the heart of the deceased. Congratulations, Ani! It looks like you can live forever in the paradise of the afterlife!

THE DEVOURER. Just as well, because the devil Ammit is ready to eat the heart of Ani if it doesn't pass the test. She has the head of a crocodile, the front part of a lion, and the back part of a hippopotamus. How frightening! The dead who end up in her jaws are said to die a second time and can never rest in peace.

En route to their eternal home

THE FUNERAL OF A PHARAOH was a very important event in the life of ancient Egypt. They celebrated 70 days after his death when the mummy was ready. Usually, preparations began many years before; when an army of specialist craftsmen ordered a vast quantity of gold and precious materials, to make coffins, a funeral mask, and furnishings fit for a king.

ON THE APPOINTED DAY, the procession crossed the Nile to the west bank in boats. The tomb was prepared on the side of the river where the sun sets. Then they disembarked and walked in procession, pulling the sarcophagus on a sled with a canopy. The procession was led by mourners, professionals responsible for showing eternal grief: they cried, wailed, waved their arms, and hurled themselves onto the ground.

THE COLOR OF MOURNING for the Egyptians was white. This is what priests, nobles, officials, the widow of the King, and the heir to the throne wore for the occasion. Along the way, muu dancers performed ritual dances with moves that had very strict rules.

SERVANTS carried funerary objects with everything the deceased needed for his new life in the afterlife. In the case of Tutankhamun, the possessions

included: jewelry, weapons, and rich furniture; but also fans, bottles of perfume, clothes, and shoes—including 27 pairs of gloves and 93 pairs of sandals; musical instruments, models of boats to travel through the underworld, and items for personal use such as a shaving kit or a first aid kit. Oh, and there were also several board games to while away the time as eternity is very long!

THEY ALSO DIDN'T FORGET food for the dead person, as his spirit had to feed itself: they put wheat and barley, several types of bread, cooked meat, onions, lentils, chickpeas, peas, dates, honey, wine, even spices to season dishes—what a banquet!

WHEN THEY ARRIVED AT THE TOMB, the priests performed sacred rituals and prayers, made offerings to the gods, burned incense, and poured water. Then they performed the ceremony of opening the mouth. Normally, the son of the deceased was responsible for touching the mouth, eyes, and ears of the mummy with a special instrument like an adze (similar to an axe). They believed that this ritual restored the senses to the mummy. So, the deceased could see, hear, and eat in the afterlife. Once completed, they put the sarcophagus in the burial chamber and sealed the tomb. Goodbye Pharaoh, safe journey!

Scenes from the afterlife

The burial chamber where they placed the king's sarcophagus was called "the Golden Room." Gold was a symbol of immortality because it never lost its brilliance. On the walls of Tutankhamun's tomb, they painted scenes of the journey to the afterlife on a layer of yellow color that represented this metal. How beautiful!

AS TUTANKHAMUN died unexpectedly, the artists had to work quickly, and in a very small space. They sealed the tomb when the paintings were still fresh. Because of that, today we can see that the walls are covered in small round brown stains. Microbes that lived happily in the warm, dark environment caused them. What you see here are the paintings archaeologists saw when they entered the burial chamber from the anteroom. They show three scenes that follow one

after the other, which are "read" backwards: the last one is really the first one…

ON THE RIGHT we see Ay, Tutankhamun's old advisor, now the new pharaoh, performing the ceremony of the "opening of the mouth" on the mummy of the dead king. Ay is dressed in a leopard skin which was worn by Sem priests. He wears a

blue crown called a Khepresh. However, the mummy looks like Osiris, the divine king of the afterlife. A large scarab beetle hangs from his necklace, another symbol of rebirth. A small table with the objects necessary for the ceremony and containers of incense is placed between the two figures.

IN THE CENTER, Tutankhamun is dead but dressed as if he were alive. He wears a wig with a gold band, a luxurious necklace, and a white loincloth. In his right hand he carries a cane; and in his left is a mace and an ankh, the symbol of life. Nut, the goddess of heaven, receives him. On her hands are the hieroglyph for water, which reads as "nyny": welcome!

ON THE LEFT of the painting is Osiris who receives Tutankhamun into his kingdom of the dead. His green skin represents two things: the fact that he is dead and also his role in the rebirth of plants, thanks to the flooding of the Nile. The pharaoh arrives wearing other clothes, accompanied by his ka wearing a false beard and carrying an ankh (a symbol of life) in its hand.

Tombs for all tastes

The ancient Egyptians put a lot of creativity and effort into designing the best home possible for the eternal rest of their dead. Here you can see how they developed these surprising constructions.

1 THE MASTABA
Originally, important people were buried in underground chambers that were accessed by a well. Then they were covered with a rectangular structure made of stone or baked clay bricks. In this part was the funerary temple where they performed the ceremonies for the dead and deposited offerings..

The Great Pyramid of Cheops in Giza was the largest building in the entire world for thousands of years. It is 755 feet long at the base and 482 feet high. It is made with 2.3 million gigantic blocks of stone: each one weighs 2.5 tons.

They shaped the blocks with very simple tools: copper chisels and wooden mallets. Then they tied them with ropes onto a kind of wooden sled...by hand!

2 THE TIERED PYRAMID
Later, one pharaoh decided that the first floor of his pyramid should be much bigger and that he would add five more levels on top, each one smaller. The result was 203 feet high, and it looked like a gigantic set of stairs reaching to the sky! That was the first pyramid in history. It is in Saqqara and was used to bury King Djoser more than 4,000 years ago and its architect was the wise Imhotep.

3 THE PYRAMIDS To the pharaohs that followed, this seemed like a very good idea and the technique was perfected very quickly. Today, the remains of 100 pyramids remain in Egypt. Would you like to know how they were built? Well, Egyptologists would like to know too! Even today, we don't know exactly how the Egyptians managed to lift those blocks of stone. To place the blocks, they probably built long earth ramps that they dismantled as the construction progressed. And, as you can imagine, it needed a huge workforce. Farmers worked on it in the summer when the Nile waters rose and flooded the fields. They were usually happy to do it because the pharaoh was a god to them, and it was also a way to pay taxes. Sometimes there were more than 40,000 on the same site. All that effort, sweat, and shouting under the merciless desert sun...

4 TOMBS IN THE ROCK
In the end, the pharaohs stopped building pyramids: they attracted too much attention and thieves always found a way in! They preferred to find a more discreet place to be buried—The Valley of the Kings. They excavated very deep tombs in the walls of the rock with lots of rooms and passages. And all the walls were magnificently decorated with paintings.

Grave robbers

Everyone knew that when the wealthy died, they were buried with mountains of treasure and the tombs were very tempting. So, the architects of tombs racked their brains to find ways for their masters to rest in eternal peace. They designed ingenious locks, false passages, sliding trapdoors, wells, and other tricks to deceive or trap whoever dared to desecrate them.

TO CREATE AN IMPENETRABLE SPACE, they usually placed a "magic brick" made of clay on each side of the burial chamber with protection spells. A curse told the potential looter: "In the water, the crocodile and the hippopotamus will be against you, on land the snake and the scorpion will be against you." Gulp! But it seems that this didn't worry too many thieves because it is extremely rare for archaeologists to find an intact tomb, or almost, like the tomb of Tutankhamun.

DESECRATING TOMBS was common practice. So much so, that thieves often counted on the collaboration of priests, scribes, and soldiers who looked the other way for a juicy bribe. Bands of thieves were well organized. They had boats to cross the river, quarry workers to open tunnels, traders to sell items on the black market, and specialists in melting down precious metals.

WE KNOW THAT THE TREASURE in the tomb of Sobekemsaf II—not an important pharaoh—was equal to almost 4.4 pounds of gold per thief. This is more than a thousand times what a laborer earned in a year. But these large gains were tied to huge risk and to attempt it required a cool head. A team of military police, the Medjay, patrolled the desert and protected the Valley of the Kings. They took dogs on their patrols ... even ferocious baboons!

THE PUNISHMENTS for thieves caught red-handed were terrible. First, they beat them with canes on the soles of their feet. Then they were condemned to death and skewered on a sharpened wooden stake ... Even so, thieves entered the tomb of Tutankhamun twice. The first time, they took oils, cloth, and small pieces of jewelry. However, the second time they were interrupted. So, their bad luck was our good fortune!

Gods everywhere

Astonished by the wonders of the world, the ancient Egyptians imagined that behind every natural phenomenon was a god or goddess with great power. Here, we introduce some of the most important, although there were thousands.

THE INHABITANTS OF THE NILE believed that order in the universe was in great danger. The forces of chaos were a constant threat and to avoid the destruction of the world it was essential to help the gods maintain balance between good and evil. So, rituals and religious ceremonies were important. And that was why the pharaoh was so important; he was the messenger between the human and divine worlds.

THE PHARAOH COUNTED ON THE HELP of many priests and priestesses for this task. There were temples in most towns and cities, but as they were considered the houses of the gods, normal people couldn't enter. Every day, the servants of the temples washed the statues of the gods, oiled and perfumed them, then dressed them luxuriously before making suitable offerings. Yes, even the statues had to eat and drink every day!

IN REALITY, the gods were a great mystery. So, they were often shown with human bodies but the head of an animal according to their powers. In this scene from the tomb of Ramesses III, the king presents an offering to Osiris, one of the most loved gods. He is shown as a mummified pharaoh: he has green skin to show he is dead. Behind him, his wife extends her protective wings. Isis was the queen of magic and had great power...

Amun:
God of the heavens and creation, one of the most important along with Osiris.

Ra:
The midday sun was another of the principal gods with the head of a falcon.

Hathor:
Great goddess of protection with a headdress of cows' horns and a solar disk.

Horus:
Son of Isis and Osiris, a god with the head of a falcon and the royal red and white crown.

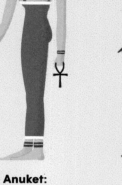

Anhur:
The patron of the Egyptian army, watched over the hunt and war.

Anuket:
The goddess of the Nile cataracts wore a crown of reeds.

Sobek:
The crocodile god of fertility and vegetation, he had a great protective power.

Maat:
She represents truth, justice, and cosmic harmony, wears a feather.

Ptah:
A creator god, sage, and healer; patron of architects and craftsmen.

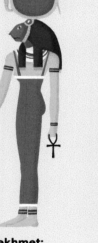

Sekhmet:
A symbol of strength and power, goddess of war and vengeance with the head of a lion.

Tueris:
With the appearance of a female hippopotamus, she is the protector of those who are pregnant.

Selket:
Goddess who prevented bites from scorpions and snakes.

Khepri:
God of the morning sun, his head is a scarab beetle.

Bastet:
With the head of a cat, she represents protection, love, and harmony.

Set:
Powerful lord of chaos. His head is a cross between a donkey and an anteater.

Tefnut:
With the head of a lion, she represents moisture, rain, and the dew that brings things to life.

Khnum:
With the head of a ram, he shaped the first humans from the clay of the Nile.

Nekhbet:
The goddess of Upper Egypt, with the head of a vulture. She also protected the pharaoh.

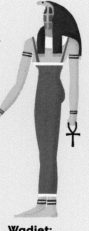

Wadjet:
Protector of Lower Egypt, with the head of a cobra.

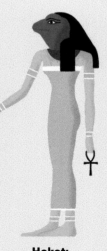

Bes:
This minor god is a dwarf with a beard and protects the home and children.

Heket:
The goddess of fertility with the head of a frog helped in childbirth

Mummies

The legend of the death and resurrection of the god Osiris was one of the main beliefs in the land of the pharaohs. As everyone wanted to guarantee eternal life in his kingdom of the afterlife, they invented this curious tradition...

THE LEGEND TELLS how Osiris was a very wise god who ruled Egypt a long time ago. But his brother Seth was very jealous and devised a plan to take his place. Using a trick, he shut him in a sarcophagus, sealed it with molten lead, and threw him into the Nile. Isis, the wife of Osiris, found the body and hid it. But Seth found it again. Filled with rage, he cut it into fourteen pieces and scattered them across the land.

ISIS DID NOT GIVE UP. She changed into a bird and flew around for years until she recovered all the pieces, one by one. Then, with the help of Anubis and Thoth, she reconstructed the body of her loved one and wrapped him in cloth. When she kissed the mummy, Osiris was reborn and became king of the afterlife. He had conquered death! So, the Egyptians worshipped him: he was proof that the cycle of life never stops...

ANUBIS was the god responsible for the process of mummification. During the funeral rituals, priests wore a jackal mask in his honor.

CANOPIC JARS housed the internal organs of the dead person. Each jar was dedicated to one of the four sons of Horus, the god of the heavens. The intestines were protected by Qebehsenuef who had the head of a falcon, the stomach by Duamutef who had the head of a jackal, the liver by Imsety who had a human head, and the lungs by Hapi who had the head of a baboon.

How was it done?

Preparing a mummy was a very meticulous and delicate process. It took 70 days, and it cost a fortune!

1 The first step was to purify the body. They washed it with natron, a mixture of salts found by the lagoons in the desert dissolved in water. Meanwhile priests recited magical spells from the sacred books.

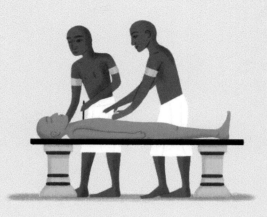

2 Then, a priest traced a line on the left side of the body and another one made a cut with a very sharp silex dagger. They took out the intestines, the liver, the stomach, and the lungs and embalmed them separately.

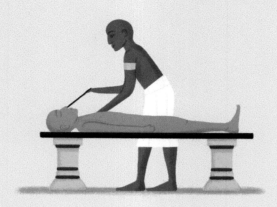

3 They did not keep the brain: they took it out in pieces through the nose with a hook. However, they left the heart in the body. They believed it was the seat of intelligence and the dead person would need it for the judgment of Osiris!

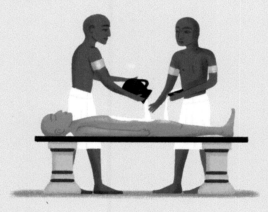

4 Once the body was emptied of its organs, it was time to dry it. They filled the abdomen with natron and covered the body with the same substance. It was left like this for 40 days and 40 nights.

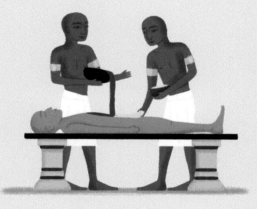

5 The body was washed to get rid of the natron and taken to the Per Nefer, the "house of mummification." There, they filled the abdomen with clay and sawdust, then smeared the body with lots of perfumes and oils to make it flexible.

6 The body was covered in liquid resin and wrapped in silk cotton strips. First, they wrapped the head, then the fingers and toes on the feet and hands, the arms and legs, and finally the trunk. This took ten days!

7 **THE FINAL TOUCHES.** The body was covered with a large piece of linen and fixed with a bandage from head to foot. The face was covered with a funerary mask that portrayed the deceased. They did this so that his ba would recognize it.

8 **THE LAST GOODBYE.** Then the body was placed in a sarcophagus in the shape of a mummy. Many prayers and magical incantations were written inside it. Just before the burial, the ceremony of the opening of the mouth assured that the dead person could breathe, speak, and eat in the afterlife. What luck!

The Valley of the Kings, my second home

The pharaohs chose a hidden valley in the Theban hills to excavate their tombs. Seen from the outside, the El Qurn peak looks like a natural pyramid. In theory, the narrow entrances to the area would make a good vantage point to catch grave robbers...

ARCHAEOLOGISTS had been working in the valley since the 19th century. In 1902, the American millionaire, Theodore Davis, was given permission to excavate there exclusively. His team discovered 35 tombs—all very interesting, but all looted! Twelve years later, thinking there was nothing else to discover, he left.

DURING HIS WORK, Davis found things relating to Tutankhamun. A small alabaster statue and a broken wooden box with fragments of gold leaf and his name inscribed on it. Also pieces of beautifully painted urns, linen headdresses, necklaces made with flowers—materials that had been used in the King's funeral ceremony. Those traces convinced me that the pharaoh must also be buried in the Valley of the Kings, and I would find him!

IN 1914, when I had everything ready, World War I broke out. What bad luck! We could only do isolated bits of work until, in August 1917, we were able to begin the first real excavation campaign. But where should we start? The Valley was full of mountains of debris from previous excavations. And there was no map to show where they had worked and where they hadn't...

I DREW A TRIANGLE between three tombs that had already been excavated and we started working enthusiastically. We had to move the rubble to get to the rock underneath. It was a desperate task, but I felt that there was a tomb there. Would we succeed in finding Tutankhamun's resting place?

A tomb appears!

Between 1917 and 1922, my army of Egyptian workers had moved hundreds of tons of sand and gravel. Yet no significant discoveries appeared to reward our effort. My patron, Lord Carnarvon, was very wealthy but he was disappointed. So much money invested—for nothing!

HE WANTED TO ABANDON IT, but I was still hopeful. I even told him I would pay for the work myself ... In the end, I convinced him to continue for one more season. Of course, he said, but only one more. That was my last opportunity!

I DECIDED TO EXCAVATE beneath the remains of huts for ancient Egyptian workers who had built the tomb of Ramses IV. By November 1, I had already contracted all the workers. Two days later, we discovered all the huts. We sketched plans and notes to be able to continue excavating beneath them. When I arrived on day 4, I found that everyone had stopped and there was total silence...

Something important had happened. Beneath the first hut, a gap had appeared in the rock. We continued to dig and in the afternoon of day 5 it was clear that there were steps that descended: the entrance to a tomb!

BUT PERHAPS we were dealing with an unfinished tomb, or one that had been looted. We held our breath and continued excavating. After step 16, the upper part of a door appeared. It was sealed! There was no name on the seal, only the symbol of the royal necropolis: a jackal with nine captives. It was the tomb of someone very important, that much was clear...

2: Ramses IV
8: Merenptah
7: Ramses II
4: Ramses XI
9: Ramses VI
6: Ramses IX
57: Horemheb
62: **Tutankhamun**
35: Amenhotep II
17: Seti I
11: Ramses III
Tumba 48
Fosa 54
20: Hatshepsut
38: Thutmose I
47: Siptah
15: Seti II
43: Thutmose IV
34: Thutmose III

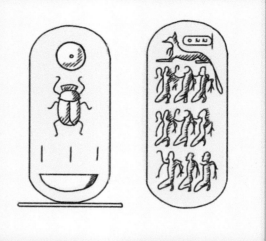

THEN I OPENED A SMALL HOLE in the mysterious door. I passed a lamp through and saw there was a passageway behind it that was filled to the roof with sand and gravel. That tomb had been well protected! I had to stop myself breaking the door down right then because it was almost nightfall. I chose the workers I trusted most and left them to guard the tomb. The following day, I sent a telegram to Lord Carnarvon: "At last have made wonderful discovery in valley. A magnificent tomb with seals intact. Re-covered same for your arrival. Congratulations." In the meantime, we had covered the entrance so well that at times I thought I had dreamed it all!

WHEN LORD CARNARVON finally arrived from England with his daughter, Lady Evelyn Herbert, it was the 24th of November. We uncovered the door again and then we realized that part of it had been opened and closed on two occasions. We knew then that grave robbers had entered but hadn't taken everything because it had been sealed again! What would be inside?

The discovery of the century

That last desperate effort in the 1922 campaign led us to a discovery we could never have dreamed of. Behind the passage and a second door appeared the almost intact tomb of Tutankhamun—and its fabulous treasure!

THE 26TH OF NOVEMBER was a great day, the most marvelous day I have ever lived. We spent the whole day emptying the passage. At midday, a second sealed door appeared, almost identical to the first. It had also been broken, then sealed again.

I OPENED A TINY HOLE at the top on the left. My hands shook. That was when I pushed my candle through, and the interior details emerged little by little from the darkness: the little room looked like a museum. It was full of objects piled one on top of the other, almost to the roof. I saw bright, golden surfaces, faces of animals projecting monstrous shadows on the wall, urns and caskets with exquisite inlaid work, beautiful furniture, and a puzzling pile of dismantled carriages shining with gold. How marvelous!

THE NEXT DAY, we installed electric light and finally entered the tomb. Imagine the intense emotions we felt—happiness at the discovery and curiosity to see everything waiting for us inside. More than 3,000 years had passed since the last time anyone had stepped inside.

BUT WE COULDN'T SEE A SARCOPHAGUS OR A MUMMY: what if it was a secret room and not a tomb? Then, between two large statues that seemed to be guardians, we saw a sealed wall. We realized that we were only at the beginning, and we would find the pharaoh farther on! We had to stop ourselves from opening it up right then. First, we needed to photograph everything, empty the chamber, and classify the items scientifically. There were dozens of them, and they were all fantastic: just one of them would have made the pain of excavating for a whole year worthwhile.

THEN WE DISCOVERED THE ANNEX—left in chaos by grave robbers, the burial chamber where Tutankhamun was buried, and finally the treasure chamber that you see here. You'll find a detailed drawing on the following pages. Every corner was filled with piles of amazing items. No one had ever found anything like it!

What a job!

No one had ever found so many wonders in one place and I wanted to be very careful. The task of conserving all of Tutankhamun's treasures was a long and delicate task: emptying the tomb took ten years! But just remember, there were 5,398 items.

I SUPERVISED all the work personally and made great efforts to make sure all the items were thoroughly catalogued. Before touching anything, we placed a small label by each item with its number and we photographed every corner of the chamber methodically. So, we always knew the position of each item, just as we found it! Then I sketched each of the pieces myself and noted down all the inscriptions they had on them so that other experts could begin deciphering what the hieroglyphics said.

ONCE DONE, the treasures were moved on stretchers padded with bandages. As everything was very delicate, we couldn't go very far. So, we converted the empty tomb of Seti II into our laboratory. It was at the back of the valley, protected from the sun and closed to tourists. There, my colleagues cleaned the items, took exact measurements, and made notes of everything on cards which were carefully filed. A catalog of wonders!

We began work in December 1922 and the last items arrived in Cairo in spring 1932. Taking the mummy out of the sarcophagus was one of the most laborious tasks. Can you imagine what a huge responsibility it was?

We were 465 miles from civilization, and we needed to be very careful not to run out of materials. To wrap the pieces, we used 32 bales of calico, one mile of wadding, and one mile of surgical bandages.

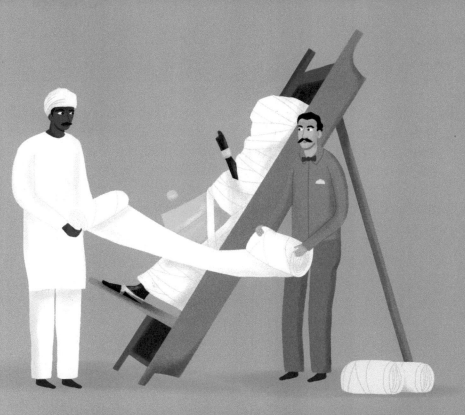

BESIDES, JUST THINK that most of the materials were very fragile. They had been waiting for us for thousands of years! If we weren't careful, many items could have disintegrated in our hands in an instant. As the environment in the tomb was very humid, the cloth, linen, and leather items would have decomposed. And those made of wood did not deal well with sudden contact with the dry desert air. On many pieces, the wood shrunk and separated from the plaster and gold sheets that covered them. Everything would have to be restored!

WE DID THE MOST URGENT REPAIRS in the desert. The rest were taken care of by the museum in Cairo. We wrapped the pieces carefully and they were moved on trams on rails toward the Nile. We had to push them for 5 miles across the desert—fifteen hours under a scorching sun!—to put them on board a ship destined for the Egyptian capital...

134

Every time we moved a piece, curious people gathered to watch us walk by. A group of armed soldiers escorted us so that no thief decided to attack us along the way!

An amazing treasure

Tutankhamun's funerary treasures have an incalculable value, but in those days, it was thought to have had a value of more than £2 million. The Egyptian government kept it all, but paid £35,000 to the heirs of Lord Carnarvon as compensation for the fortune that had been spent on finding the tomb...

▲ Imagine how this ceremonial chariot, covered in gold, must have shone under the Egyptian sun! Its wooden structure was delicately curved, and the six-spoked wheels had leather "tires."

▲ A lot of skill was needed to make this bottle of perfumed oil. And a lot of work! It is carved in calcite and decorated with enameled and gold-colored porcelain.

▼ Among the 35 models of boats, there were boats for all occasions: papyrus boats for traveling on the delta, solar boats for journeys by night, and boats to accompany the sun god...

► The Ushabtis were magical servants for work in the future life. In total, there were 413 small figurines of all kinds: wood, enameled porcelain, stone...

◄ Scepters and fans were an important symbol of power for the pharaoh. Imagine the fan covered in alternating white and brown ostrich feathers. Very stylish!

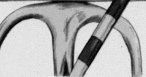

► Perhaps the falcon pendant with extended wings was one of the favorite jewels of the king: it was found in the deepest bandages of the mummy. It is gold and engraved on a green stone.

▼ On the back of this throne covered in gold leaf is Tutankhamun and his queen depicted with silver and other inlays.

▼ One of the favorite pastimes of the ancient Egyptians was senet, a board game. This wooden board is decorated with marble squares, some touches of gold, and lions' feet at the bottom of the legs. Wow!

▲ The full-sized guardian represents the ka of Tutankhamun who, with his stick and his mace, protected the burial chamber and its precious contents. It was made of wood covered in plaster.

► Amongst the almost 100 pairs of shoes in the tomb, these wooden sandals trimmed with leather stand out. They have images of enemy prisoners on the soles so that the pharaoh stepped all over them when he walked!

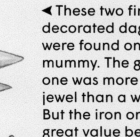

◄ These two finely decorated daggers were found on the mummy. The gold one was more of a jewel than a weapon. But the iron one had great value because the Egyptians didn't know how to forge this metal.

◄ This pectoral showing the goddess Nut is an exceptional piece. The base is a gold plaque with inlays of carnallite and colored crystals. On the back, there are many religious texts in hieroglyphs.

Inside the tomb

Here is an exact reproduction of the tomb of the young pharaoh as we found it in 1922. The truth is that, compared to other tombs in the Valley of the Kings, it's tiny. Perhaps it was excavated for someone less important; and as Tutankhamun died sooner than expected, they had to use it in a hurry. But never in such a small place—it measured only 1,184 square feet—had so many fabulous treasures been crammed together: there were 5,398 items!

PILES OF THINGS
In the second chamber, which we called the annex, there were more than 2,000 items in messy piles over six feet high. It was chaotic! Among them, we found 116 containers of food, 30 clay jars of wine, and several senet boards, the favorite game of the ancient Egyptians.

ETERNAL REST
These three magnificent funerary litters were part of the equipment that the king would use to be reborn in the afterlife. Various sacred animals are carved on its legs.

THE ANNEX

THE ANTECHAMBER

WOODEN STATUE
It seems likely that this statue of the pharaoh without legs was a kind of mannequin. It served to organize the king's clothes and jewelry that he had to wear each day!

LUXURIOUS VEHICLES
Four chariots, dismantled so that they fitted into such a small space, were mounted on the walls. One was for war, another for hunting, and two for parades, each coated in gold and beautifully decorated.

TRACES OF GRAVE ROBBERS
Among the 700 plus items, we found piles of food offerings, the remains of floral decorations, and baskets from the time of the burial in the antechamber. But there was also debris and broken porcelain that grave robbers left behind.

THE FUNERARY MASK is pure gold and weighs 5.5 pounds. It has delicate inlays of colored crystals and various minerals: carnelian, lapis lazuli, quartz, and obsidian. That's why it is one of the best-known treasures of ancient Egypt.

THE FACE of the pharaoh was shaped with hammers on two overlapping sheets of gold. Afterwards, they added ears and a false beard. At the top is a vulture and a cobra made of pure gold. They represent Nekhbet and Wadjet, the goddesses of Upper and Lower Egypt.

THE NECKLACE has twelve alternating rows of inlays in red and blue. Pieces in the shape of a falcon's head cover the shoulders. On the back of the mask, a spell asks the goddesses to protect each of the features of the king's face. Such detail!

3,000 years of history... and records!

Tutankhamun's treasure is the most spectacular in Ancient Egypt. But as the pharaonic civilization lasted for so long, there was time for many more surprising events to take place and they made some amazing buildings...

THE LARGEST KINGDOM

Some chronicles suggest Pharaoh Pepi II had a 90-year reign, but most experts doubt this figure is true. They think it is more likely he was on the throne for some 64 years. If that was so, the longest reign is that of Ramses III, which is well documented. This warrior pharaoh and great builder of temples governed for 66 years and died having celebrated his 90th birthday. He had numerous wives and over 100 children.

DID WOMEN RULE?

During the 3,000 years of history in ancient Egypt, there were approximately 170 pharaohs, but only 19 of them were women! They reigned until their sons were old enough to take the throne. Clearly, pharaonic society thought power was for men, but some women showed they were perfectly capable of governing. The most famous were Hatshepsut, Nefertiti, Twosret, and Cleopatra VII!

GODDESSES ON EVERY CORNER

It isn't known for certain how many goddesses were worshipped by the ancient Egyptians, but there were a lot! The North American Egyptologist, James Peter Allen, specialist in pharaonic religion, reckons that hieroglyphic texts mention more than 1,400 different goddesses. You have to bear in mind that many parts of the country had their own protective goddesses just for that place. Remembering them all must have been a complicated task, even for priests!

THE BEST TEMPLE OF ALL

The complex at Karnac, dedicated to the gods Amun, Mut, and Khonsu, is in Thebes on the banks of the Nile. Some 30 pharaohs contributed to the splendor of the complex, adding ever more spectacular and carefully decorated buildings. It covers an area of 0.39 square miles and the most spectacular building is the Great Hypostyle Hall. Its 134 columns are very tall and are covered in hieroglyphs from top to bottom!

THE LARGEST BUILDING
To build the pyramid at Cheops, the largest of the three at Giza, 2,300,000 blocks of stone were used. Each block weighs some 2.5 tons and the whole pyramid weighs 6 million tons. Incredible! Egyptian astronomers oriented it so that its four sides look precisely north, south, east, and west. It's as if it were the exact center of the earth!

THE MOST BRUTAL BATTLE
In the year 1479 BC, between 10,000 and 20,000 soldiers under the command of Pharaoh Thutmose III faced their enemies. It happened that a coalition of kings from the Near East had rebelled by not paying tributes to those who collected them on behalf of the Pharaoh. The Egyptians achieved a great victory in the battle of Megiddo and then besieged the city for seven months until it surrendered. Thanks to Thutmose III and his warriors, the Egyptian empire achieved the largest expansion of its territory.

EVEN LONGER PAPYRI!
The Harris Papyrus is the longest ever preserved: it measures 134.5 feet, and it deals with religious and historical themes. The Diary of Merer (who was a foreman for boat owners), is the oldest papyrus to be discovered: it is some 4,500 years old! The Ebers Papyrus is one of the oldest preserved medical texts: it is 3,500 years old! It is more than 66 feet long and its 877 sections describe a multitude of illnesses and remedies using hundreds of plants.

THE FIRST STRIKE
On November 14, 1152 BC, 70 craftsmen working in the Valley of the Kings said they had had enough: "we're hungry and 18 days have passed ... we came here because of hunger and thirst; we have no clothes, no fish, no vegetables. Ask this of the pharaoh, our great lord, and the vizier, our master, that they give us food." It is the first time in history that we know that a worker confronted his master and fought for his rights!